Mocktails

A DELICIOUS COLLECTION OF NON-ALCOHOLIC DRINKS

This book features more than 50 delicious mocktail recipes perfect for any occasion. Whether you are hosting a party or just looking for a refreshing non-alcoholic drink, these mocktails will hit the spot. So grab your shaker and get mixing!

Moira Clark

FOLLOW THESE STEPS TO CLAIM YOUR <u>FREE GIFT</u>!

- Go to your orders page and click on <u>**Write a product review**</u> and write a review for our Mocktails Recipe Book
- Take a **Screenshot** of the review
- Send us the screenshot to: **moiraclarkbooks@gmail.com**
- Specify the gift you chose and the address you want it to be shipped to.
- Done!

Round Ice Cube Tray

Stainless Still Straws Set

TABLE OF CONTENTS

INTRODUCTION

Mocktails are non-alcoholic drinks that mimic the flavors and presentation of cocktails. The main difference between mocktails and cocktails is that mocktails do not contain any alcohol, while cocktails typically include at least one type of spirit.

Mocktails can be made with a variety of ingredients, including fruit juices, soda, herbs, and spices. While some are similar to virgin versions of popular cocktails, others are unique creations that stand on their own. Many mocktails are brightly colored and garnished with fruit or other decorations.

The flavor profile of a mocktail is often complex, with a balance of sweet, sour, and savory elements. They can be enjoyed by people of all ages and are a popular choice for designated drivers, pregnant women, and those who are avoiding alcohol for other reasons.

Whether you're looking for a refreshing summer sipper or a festive holiday mocktail, there's sure to be a recipe to suit your taste.

The history of mocktails and their rise in popularity is interesting. Mocktails have been around for centuries, but they gained popularity in the United States during the Prohibition era. Since alcohol was illegal, people began to experiment with ways to recreate their favorite cocktails without using spirits.

Mocktails continued to be popular throughout the years, but they experienced a resurgence in recent years as more people are looking for ways to enjoy the flavors of cocktails without the alcohol.

If you're interested in making your own mocktails at home, there are a few things you'll need.

Some basic bartending supplies are essential. You'll need a shaker, strainer, jigger, and stirrer. You'll also need some glassware. Collins glasses, martini glasses, and highball glasses are all good choices.

TOOLS

We have made a list of the tools and glassware we have used to create the mocktails in this book.

Feel free to check them out as a reference by scanning the **QR Code below**.

SYRUPS

STRAWBERRY ORANGE GINGER SYRUP

INGREDIENTS

- 8 ounces strawberries, hulled and quartered
- 3 inches of fresh ginger, peeled and sliced
- Three 3-inch strips of orange peel, removed with a vegetable peeler
- 1/3 cup honey
- 1/4 cup fresh-squeezed orange juice
- 1/4 cup water
- Pinch of sea salt

PREPARATION

1. Place all the ingredients in a small saucepan over medium heat.
2. Bring to a boil and then simmer for about five minutes.
3. Let the syrup cool down, then strain it into a bowl or jar, using a spoon to extract as much syrup as possible.
4. Allow the syrup to cool down even more until it reaches room temperature before making a drink. You can store it for up to one week in the fridge.

BLACKBERRY SYRUP

INGREDIENTS

- 6 ounces blackberries
- 1/4 cup honey
- 1/4 cup water
- 1/2 teaspoon vanilla extract
- Pinch of salt

PREPARATION

1. In a small saucepan place all the ingredients and cook over medium-low heat for about 10-15 minutes, stirring occasionally.
2. Let it cool down and then blend it with an immersion (or regular) blender.
3. Pour the syrup through a fine-mesh strainer to remove all the seeds.
4. Let the syrup cool down to room temperature before using it for a drink.

BLUEBERRY GINGER SYRUP

INGREDIENTS

- 1-liter water
- 1 1/4 cups fresh blueberries
- 1 tbsp of grated ginger
- 4-5 tbsp of sugar

PREPARATION

1. In a pan add blueberries, water and grated ginger. Leave it on medium heat and bring it to a boil.
2. When it is boiling, add the sugar and stir it until it dissolves completely.
3. Once the sugar is dissolved, lower the heat, and using a potato masher, crush the blueberries. Let the mixture rest for another 15 minutes.
4. Remove from the heat and when the syrup cools down cover it with the lid and let it rest for 3 more hours. This is an important step because it helps the flavors to mix as best as possible.
5. After 3 hours, pour the syrup into a bottle or jar. It can last up to 2 weeks in the fridge.

LAVENDER SYRUP

INGREDIENTS

- 1 cup water
- ½ cup sugar
- juice of 1 lemon
- 4-6 1-2 inch sprigs of lavender

PREPARATION

1. Combine the lavender, water, and sugar in a small saucepan.
2. Add the lemon juice. Bring the mixture to a boil over medium-high heat then reduce the heat to low and simmer for 25-30 minutes until the liquid has reduced and the mixture has thickened.
3. Strain it into a jar with a fine-mesh strainer.
4. Use a spatula or spoon to press on the solids and extract all the syrup. Allow the syrup to cool down to room temperature and then store in the fridge for up to a week.

MINT SIMPLE SYRUP

INGREDIENTS

- 1/2 cup granulated sugar
- 1/2 cup water
- 3 sprigs mint

PREPARATION

1. In a pan, add sugar and water over medium heat.
2. Stir often until sugar is completely dissolved (about 3-4 minutes).
3. Remove from heat and add mint sprigs. Let sit for at least 30 minutes.
4. Power the syrup in a jar. It will last for about a week in the refrigerator.

RASPBERRY SYRUP

INGREDIENTS

- 1 ½ cups of raspberries (fresh or frozen)
- 1 cup of white granulated sugar
- ¾ cups of water

PREPARATION

1. In a small pot, add all ingredients.
2. Stir it together and bring it to a boil. Once it is boiling, reduce the heat and simmer for 10 minutes, until the raspberries start breaking down. Strain the syrup through a fine-mesh strainer.
3. Let the syrup cool down and then pour it into a jar or bottle and keep it in the fridge for up to 2 weeks.

ORANGE SYRUP

INGREDIENTS

- 8 oz water
- 8 oz granulated sugar
- 3 oranges, sliced

PREPARATION

1. In a saucepan, combine the water, sugar, and orange peels. Stir to combine.
2. Bring to a boil and cook until the sugar dissolves, stirring occasionally.
3. Remove from heat, strain out the peels, and let the syrup cool down.
4. Transfer to a bottle and refrigerate for up to 2 weeks.

ROSE SYRUP

INGREDIENTS

- ¾ cup of water
- ¾ cup of sugar
- ¼ cup of dried rose petals

PREPARATION

1. Put all ingredients in a small pan and let it simmer.
2. Stir occasionally to make sure sugar dissolves completely.
3. Take off the heat and let it cool down for 15 minutes.
4. Strain and pour the syrup into a jar or bottle.
5. keep it refrigerated for up to 2 weeks.

CHAMOMILE SYRUP

INGREDIENTS

- 1 cup granulated sugar
- ½ cup filtered water
- 3 individual bags of chamomile tea

PREPARATION

1. Place sugar and water in a small pan and set over medium heat.
2. Bring to a simmer, until the sugar dissolves, stirring occasionally, for about 5 minutes.
3. Remove from heat and add the tea bags.
4. let it rest for 10 minutes, then discard tea bags. Let it cool down and then transfer it into a jar. It can be stored in the fridge for up to 2 weeks.

GINGER SIMPLE SYRUP

INGREDIENTS

- 3/4 cup of sugar
- 3/4 cup of water
- 1/3 cup of peeled and chopped ginger

PREPARATION

1. In a small pan, add the sugar, water and ginger and bring to a boil, stirring occasionally to make sure the sugar dissolves completely.
2. Remove from the heat and let it rest for 20-30 minutes.
3. Strain into a jar. Keep refrigerated for up to 2 weeks.

CHERRY SYRUP

INGREDIENTS

- 16 Ounces Cherries, (frozen, pitted)
- 1 Cup Granulated Sugar
- 1 Cup Water
- ½ oz. Lemon Juice

PREPARATION

1. In a medium pan, place the cherries, sugar, water, and lemon juice. Bring to a simmer over low-medium heat and stir occasionally to make sure the sugar dissolves completely. Use a potato masher to take out all the flavor from the cherries. Let me syrup simmer for 8 to 10 minutes until the fruit has completely broken down.
2. Remove from heat, and let the mixture cool down for 15 minutes. strain the syrup with a fine mesh to remove all the fruit pieces.
3. Keep in the refrigerator for up to 2 weeks.

GINGER–LIME SYRUP

INGREDIENTS

- 1/2 cup ginger juice
- 1/2 cup lime juice
- 1 cup turbinado sugar

PREPARATION

1. Put all ingredients in a saucepan and simmer.
2. Stir to make sure sugar dissolves completely.
3. Take off heat and steep for 15 minutes.
4. Strain the syrup and pour it into a jar or bottle.
5. keep refrigerated for up to 2 weeks.

ORANGE GRAPEFRUIT SYRUP

INGREDIENTS

- ½ grapefruit
- 1 orange slice
- 1 cup of caster sugar
- 1 cup of Water
- 3 Cardamom pods, lightly crushed
- Pinch coriander seeds

PREPARATION

1. Chop the grapefruit into small pieces and put them into a pan. Then add the orange slice, sugar, water, cardamom pods, and coriander seeds.
2. Bring it to a simmer on medium heat and cook for 5 minutes. crush the fruit with a spoon as it starts to soften while cooking.
3. Take it off the heat and let it cool down.
4. Once it cooled down, strain it and discard the fruit pieces.
5. Store in the fridge for up to one week.

RHUBARB SYRUP

INGREDIENTS

- 3 cups of water
- 2 cups of chopped rhubarb
- 1/2 cup of honey
- 1-inch ginger grated

PREPARATION

1. Place all of the ingredients into a small pot and bring it to a boil.
2. When it boils, lower the heat and let it simmer for 15 minutes.
3. After 15 minutes remove from heat.
4. Let the mixture cool down for 20 minutes.
5. After the mixture cools down, strain the syrup into a jar or bottle.
6. Refrigerate for up to 2 weeks.

RHUBARB ROSEMARY SYRUP

INGREDIENTS

- 2 cups of chopped rhubarb
- 1/2 cup of honey
- 3 cups of water
- 2 sprigs of fresh rosemary

PREPARATION

1. In a large pan, add the honey, chopped rosemary, rhubarb, and water.
2. Bring it to a boil, then let it simmer for 30 minutes.
3. After it rested, strain the syrup into a bottle or jar with a fine mesh to take out all the solid pieces.
4. keep refrigerated for up to one week.

SIMPLE SYRUP

INGREDIENTS

- 1/2 cup granulated sugar
- 1/2 cup water

PREPARATION

1. Add the sugar and water to a small pan over medium heat.
2. Stir until sugar is completely dissolved.
3. Let it cool down, then pour it into a jar.
4. Keep refrigerated for up to a month.

STRAWBERRY SYRUP 🍓

INGREDIENTS

- 8 oz strawberries, stems removed and sliced (1.5 cups, measured)
- 1 cup water
- 1 cup granulated sugar

PREPARATION

1. In a pan, combine the strawberries, water, and sugar over medium-high heat.
2. Bring to a boil, then reduce to low heat, and cook for 20 minutes, until the syrup is red.
3. Take out the strawberries from the syrup, making sure not to press down on the strawberries.
4. Let the syrup cool down for about an hour.
5. keep refrigerated for up to one week.

BASIL SIMPLE SYRUP

INGREDIENTS

- 1 cup water
- 1 cup white sugar
- 1 cup fresh basil leaves

PREPARATION

1. In a small pan, add water, sugar, and basil leaves.
2. Bring to a boil, stirring occasionally until sugar dissolves completely.
3. Remove from heat and let the syrup rest for at least 30 minutes.
4. With a mesh strainer, pour the syrup into a jar or bottle.
5. Keep refrigerated for up to 2 weeks.

ORGEAT SYRUP

INGREDIENTS

- 2 cups blanched almonds
- 1 1/2 cups sugar
- 1 1/4 cups water
- 1/2 teaspoon orange flower water

PREPARATION

1. Blend the almonds in a food processor until completely ground and then set aside.
2. In a small pan, add the sugar and water and stir until sugar dissolves completely over medium heat. Boil the syrup for about 3 minutes and then add the almonds you have previously set aside.
3. Simmer for another 3 minutes on low heat, then slowly increase the temperature to medium-high. Before it starts to boil, remove it from the heat and cover it with a lid.
4. Keep it covered for at least 3 hours and up to 8. After, strain it through cheesecloth, removing all the ground almonds.
5. Add the orange flower water to the syrup.
6. Pour the syrup into a jar or bottle.
7. Keep refrigerated for up to 2 weeks.

MASALA CHAI SYRUP ✳

INGREDIENTS

- ¾ cup of water
- ¾ cup of maple syrup
- 2 cinnamon sticks
- 2 tbsp of cardamom pods
- 1 star of anise
- 2 inches of sliced fresh ginger
- 1 tbsp of black peppercorn
- 2 tsp of cloves

PREPARATION

1. Combine all the ingredients and put it to boil on low heat until the sugar is melted.
2. Let it simmer for at least 20 minutes and up to one hour.
3. Remove from the heat.
4. Let it cool.
5. Strain the syrup into a bottle and store it in the fridge for up to 2 weeks.

ROSEMARY MAPLE SYRUP

INGREDIENTS

- ½ cup of Maple Syrup
- ½ cup of Water
- 4 Big springs of rosemary
- ½ tsp of Cinnamon

PREPARATION

1. In a small pan, put the water and maple syrup over medium heat.
2. Simmer for about 10 minutes.
3. Remove from the heat.
4. Let it cool down with the lid on for 30 minutes.
5. Pour the syrup into a bottle or jar.
6. Keep refrigerated for up to 2 weeks.

EARL GREY SYRUP

INGREDIENTS

- 4-6 bags of earl grey tea
- 1 cup of water
- 1 1/2 cups of granulated sugar

PREPARATION

1. Put the tea bags in boiling water for 10-15 minutes.
2. Remove tea bags and add sugar.
3. Over low heat, stir until sugar is completely dissolved.
4. Remove from heat and let it cool down.
5. Pour the syrup into a jar or bottle.
6. Keep refrigerated for up to 2 weeks.

GREEN APPLE SYRUP

INGREDIENTS

- 7 oz. Green apple cut into small pieces
- 4 cups water
- 1 ½ cups sugar
- Pinch of salt

PREPARATION

1. In a small pan, add apples and water over medium-high heat. Bring to a boil, reduce heat, and simmer for 2 hours.
2. Take out the apples and discard them.
3. In another pan add equal amounts of the apple concentrate you just made and sugar (for example, 1 cup of apple water and 1 cup of sugar).
4. Place over medium heat and cook until sugar dissolves completely, stirring occasionally without letting it boil.
5. Let it cool down for about 1 hour.
6. Pour it into a jar or bottle.
7. Keep refrigerated for up to 2 weeks.

PASSION FRUIT SYRUP

INGREDIENTS

- 1 cup of Sugar
- 1 cup of Water
- 1 cup Passion Fruit Pulp

PREPARATION

1. In a small pan, add sugar and water and bring to a boil. Stirring occasionally until sugar is dissolved completely.
2. Remove from heat.
3. Add the passion fruit pulp.
4. Let the pulp steep in the syrup for two hours.
5. Pour the syrup into a jar or bottle.
6. Keep refrigerated for up to 2 weeks.

FIG SYRUP

INGREDIENTS

- 2 cups figs washed, and cut in half
- 1/2 cup honey
- 3 cups of filtered water

PREPARATION

1. In a large pan, place all the ingredients over medium heat.
2. Bring it to a boil, then let it simmer for about 20 minutes.
3. After 20 minutes, take out the figs from the syrup.
4. Pour the syrup into a jar using a fine mesh strainer.
5. Keep refrigerated for up to 2 weeks.

RECIPES

STRAWBERRY ORANGE GINGER FIZZ

INGREDIENTS

- 1 oz. Strawberry orange ginger syrup (recipe on page 12)
- 6 oz. Sparkling water
- Ice
- 1 Orange wheel, half a hulled strawberry, and a sprig of mint, for serving

PREPARATION

1. Grab a glass and pour 2-3 tbsp of syrup into the bottom.
2. Pour sparkling water until the glass is almost full.
3. Add the Ice.
4. Garnish with an orange wheel, a strawberry and a small spring of mint.
5. Enjoy!

SCAN ME

BLACKBERRY MOCKTAIL

INGREDIENTS

- 1 wedge of lime
- 3-6 mint leaves, torn
- 1 oz. Blackberry syrup, to taste (recipe on page 13)
- Handful of ice
- 6-8 oz. club soda or seltzer
- Slice of lime, mint leaf, and blackberries for garnish

PREPARATION

1. Squeeze the lime wedge into the bottom of a glass and drop the lime into the glass.
2. Add the torn mint leaves and muddle them with the lime juice.
3. Add the blackberry syrup and then the ice, and top with club soda.
4. Garnish with a lime wheel, a mint leaf, and a blackberry or two threaded onto a cocktail pick.
5. Enjoy!

SCAN ME

BLUEBERRY GINGER MOCKTAIL

INGREDIENTS

- 2 oz. of Blueberry Ginger Syrup (recipe on page 14)
- 1 cup of lime sparkling water
- Ice cubes
- Mint leaves

PREPARATION

1. Pour the syrup into a tall glass.
2. Add the sparkling water on top and stir well.
3. Garnish with fresh blueberries and some mint leaves.
4. Enjoy!

SCAN ME

LAVENDER MOCKTAIL

INGREDIENTS

- Ice
- 2 oz. Fresh grapefruit juice
- 1 ½ oz. Lavender Syrup (recipe on page 15)
- 3-4 oz. Chilled club soda
- 1 basil sprig
- 1 fresh lavender sprig (optional)

PREPARATION

1. Fill a cocktail shaker with ice.
2. Add the lavender syrup, grapefruit juice and shake well.
3. Strain into an ice-filled collins glass, add the club soda and stir.
4. Garnish with the basil and lavender sprigs.

SCAN ME

MAPLE MOCKTAIL

INGREDIENTS

- 2 oz. Cranberry juice
- 2 oz. Apple juice
- 2 oz. Sparkling water
- 1 oz. Lemon juice
- 2 oz. Maple syrup
- Maple sugar and cinnamon stick to garnish

PREPARATION

1. Mix the 5 first ingredients in a shaker and shake it gently.
2. Dim the rim of a footed pilsner glass with maple sugar.
3. Add ice to the glass and strain the drink into the glass.
4. Garnish with a cinnamon stick.
5. Enjoy!

SCAN ME

MOJITO MOCKTAIL

INGREDIENTS

- Ice
- ½ oz. Lime juice
- 1 ½ oz. Mint simple syrup (recipe on page 16)
- 3 oz. Club soda
- Lime slices and mint sprigs for garnish

PREPARATION

1. Fill a tall glass with ice.
2. Add the syrup, lime juice and club soda.
3. Stir until well-combined.
4. Garnish with additional limes and mint
5. Enjoy!

SCAN ME

ELDERFLOWER MOCKTAIL

INGREDIENTS

- 1 oz. Raspberry Syrup (recipe on page 17)
- 1/4 oz. Lemon Juice
- 2 oz. Elderflower Tea
- Soda Water
- Ice Cubes
- 5 fresh raspberries
- Mint spring for garnish

PREPARATION

1. Pour raspberry syrup, lime juice and tea into the glass
2. Add ice cubes
3. Fill up with soda water
4. Add the fresh raspberries and garnish with mint
5. Enjoy!

SCAN ME

ORANGE ROSE MOCKTAIL

INGREDIENTS

- 1 oz. Orange Syrup (recipe on page 18)
- 1 oz. Rose Syrup (recipe on page 19)
- 1 oz. Lime Juice
- Ginger Ale
- Ice Cubes
- Orange wheel for garnish

PREPARATION

1. Pour orange syrup and lime juice into the glass.
2. Add ice cubes and then pour rose syrup.
3. Fill up with Ginger ale.
4. Garnish with an orange wheel.
5. Enjoy!

SCAN ME

AGAVE GRAPEFRUIT MOCKTAIL

INGREDIENTS

- 2 oz. Grapefruit juice
- ½ oz. Lime juice
- 1/4 oz. Agave nectar
- Pinch of cinnamon
- 1 bottle (100 ml) red bitter soda
- Sprig of rosemary for garnish

PREPARATION

1. Into a Shaking Tin, combine de Grapefruit juice, lime juice and agave nectar.
2. Add a pinch of ground cinnamon.
3. Shake it up.
4. Pour it into a collins glass with ice.
5. Mix it with 3oz of Red Bitter Soda.
6. Garnish with a spring of rosemary.
7. Enjoy!

SCAN ME

CHAMOMILE MOCKTAIL

INGREDIENTS

- 8 mint leaves
- 1 oz. Chamomile simple syrup (recipe on page 20)
- 1oz. Ginger simple syrup (recipe on page 21)
- ¼ cup of Cranberry juice
- 1 Bottle of Ginger beer

PREPARATION

1. Put the mint leaves into a shaker.
2. Add the chamomile syrup, ginger syrup and muddle.
3. Add the cranberry juice and ice.
4. Shake well.
5. Strain into a glass
6. Top with Ginger Beer
7. Enjoy!

SCAN ME

CHERRY LIME MOCKTAIL

INGREDIENTS

- 1 cup of Soda water
- 1 ½ oz. Cherry syrup (recipe on page 22)
- 1 ½ Lime Juice
- 4-5 fresh cherries
- Mint spring for garnish

PREPARATION

1. Put ice on a tall glass.
2. Add the sherry syrup and lime juice.
3. Top it with soda water and stir.
4. And the fresh cherries and garnish with the mint spring.
5. Enjoy!

SCAN ME

GINGER LIME MULE

INGREDIENTS

- 1½ oz. Ginger-lime syrup (recipe on page 23)
- 6 oz. Soda water
- Candied ginger, for garnish

PREPARATION

1. In a shaker, combine the ginger-lime syrup and soda water.
2. Stir gently, then double strain it over ice in a Collins glass.
3. Garnish with a piece of candied ginger.
4. Enjoy!

SCAN ME

GRAPEFRUIT & TONIC MOCKTAIL

INGREDIENTS

- 7-10 fresh blueberries
- 1-2 Star anise
- 1 Cucumber
- ½ Grapefruit
- 6 oz. Tonic Water
- 1 Rosemary sprig

PREPARATION

1. In a wine glass, combine the blueberries and the star anise.
2. Peel and add 3 large sections of the cucumber.
3. Peel a large section of the grapefruit and twist the rind into the glass, rub the peel on the inside and add to the glass.
4. Fill the glass with ice and add top it with quality tonic water
5. Garnish the rosemary sprig and stir the drink well using the sprig to maximize the aromatics.
6. Enjoy!

SCAN ME

NEGRONI MOCKTAIL

INGREDIENTS

- Ice
- 2 oz. Orange grapefruit syrup (recipe on page 24)
- 1 oz. White grape juice
- ½ oz. Cold water
- An Orange slice for garnish

PREPARATION

1. Add ice to a glass.
2. Pour the orange grapefruit syrup.
3. Add the white grape juice.
4. Add the cold water.
5. Garnish with an orange slice.
6. Enjoy!

SCAN ME

NEW YORK MOCKTAIL

INGREDIENTS

- 1 oz.Lemon juice
- 1 oz. Maple syrup
- 3 oz. Assam tea leaves
- 1 oz. Egg white
- Ice
- 3 oz. Pomegranate juice
- 1 Rosemary spring

PREPARATION

1. Pour the lemon juice, maple syrup, tea and egg white into a cocktail shaker.
2. Shake well until the mixture is frothy. Add a good handful of ice and shake again.
3. Double strain into a glass filled with ice.
4. Top up the pomegranate juice.
5. Garnish with the rosemary and foam left on the shaker (optional).
6. Enjoy!

SCAN ME

ORANGE LAVENDER MOCKTAIL

INGREDIENTS

- Ice
- 1 oz. Lavender syrup (recipe on page 15)
- ½ Cup of orange juice
- ½ oz. Grenadine
- Orange wheel and lavender spring for garnish

PREPARATION

1. Put the ice into a shaker.
2. Add the Lavender Syrup.
3. Add the orange juice.
4. Add the Grenadine.
5. Shake well for 5-10 seconds.
6. Pour it into a cold glass.
7. Garnish with orange wheel and lavender spring.
8. Enjoy!

SCAN ME

PEACH MOCKTAIL

INGREDIENTS

- 1 ripe peach, already cut into slices and frozen
- 1 oz. Sugar
- ½ oz. Lime juice
- ½ cup of Apple juice
- Ice
- ½ cup of Sparkling Water
- 2-4 leaves of fresh mint

PREPARATION

1. Put the peach, sugar, lime juice and apple juice in a blender.
2. Blend until the mixture is smooth.
3. Put Ice Cubes into a Glass.
4. Add mint and pour the mixture.
5. Add mint leaves.
6. Top with sparkling water and stir well.
7. Enjoy!

SCAN ME

RASPBERRY PASSION MOCKTAIL

INGREDIENTS

- 1oz. Red grapefruit juice
- 2 oz. Raspberry syrup (recipe on page 17)
- 1 cup of Soda Water
- Ice
- 5-7 raspberries
- 1 Rosemary spring

PREPARATION

1. Put the ice in a shaker.
2. Add the grapefruit juice and the raspberry syrup.
3. Shake it.
4. Put ice in the glass and pour the mixture.
5. Top with soda water.
6. Add fresh raspberries and garnish with a rosemary spring.
7. Enjoy!

SCAN ME

RHUBARB GINGER MOCKTAIL

INGREDIENTS

- Ice
- 2 oz. Rhubarb Syrup (recipe on page 25)
- 1 cup of Club Soda
- 2 Basil leaves
- 1 Basil leave and Rosemary spring for garnish.

PREPARATION

1. In a shaker add ice, the syrup, club soda and basil.
2. Stir it.
3. Strain the cocktail into a martini glass.
4. Garnish with a basil leave and rosemary spring.
5. Enjoy!

SCAN ME

ROSEMARY RHUBARB MOCKTAIL

INGREDIENTS

- 2 oz. Club soda
- 1 oz. Rhubarb rosemary simple syrup (recipe on page 26)
- Rosemary spring for garnish
- Ice

PREPARATION

1. Pour the rhubarb syrup into a tall and thin glass.
2. Top with club soda.
3. Add large ice.
4. Garnish with the rosemary spring.
5. Enjoy!

SCAN ME

THYME MOCKTAIL

INGREDIENTS

- 1 oz. Simple syrup (recipe on page 27)
- 5 Springs of fresh thyme
- 1 cup of Sparkling water
- ½ cup of Grapefruit juice
- Ice
- 1 spring of thyme for garnish

PREPARATION

1. Put the fresh thyme into a shaker and syrup.
2. Muddle the thyme.
3. Add the grapefruit juice.
4. Shake well for 5-10 seconds.
5. Put ice into a glass.
6. Strain the thyme mixture.
7. Top with Sparkling Water.
8. Garnish with a thyme spring.
9. Enjoy!

SCAN ME

WATERMELON MOCKTAIL

INGREDIENTS

- 60gr Watermelon wedges/slice
- 1 oz. Strawberry Syrup (recipe on page 28)
- 5 oz. Soda Water
- Ice
- Lime slice for garnish

PREPARATION

1. Put watermelon wedges/slices into the glass then muddle well.
2. Add the strawberry syrup and 2oz of soda water.
3. Stir well.
4. Add ice and fill up with the remaining soda
5. Garnish with lime slice.
6. Enjoy!

SCAN ME

WATERMELON MOJITO

INGREDIENTS

- Sugar to rim the glass
- 2 small lime slices
- ½ oz. Lime juice
- 1 small bunch of fresh mint
- 1 ½ oz. Simple Syrup (recipe on page 27)
- ½ Cup of watermelon, blended
- Soda water
- Ice Cubes

PREPARATION

1. Put the watermelon into a blender and mix it until smooth.
2. In a glass rimmed with sugar, put a slice of lime, mint leaves and lime juice. Muddle to take out the flavors.
3. Add the syrup and the blended watermelon. Stir well.
4. Top with Soda Water and add ice cubes
5. Garnish with a spring of mint and lime wheel
6. Enjoy!

SCAN ME

APPLE CIDER MOCKTAIL

INGREDIENTS

- 2 oz. Apple juice
- 1 oz. Apple cider vinegar
- ½ oz. Maple syrup
- ½ Cup ginger beer, chilled
- Ice
- Slice of apple and star anise to garnish

PREPARATION

1. Mix together apple juice, vinegar, and maple syrup in a shaker.
2. Shake it.
3. Put ice in a cup and pour the ginger beer.
4. Pour the mix from the shaker.
5. Garnish with the apple slice and anise.
6. Enjoy!

SCAN ME

BASIL MARTINI MOCKTAIL

INGREDIENTS

- 4 oz. Lemon juice
- 2 oz. Basil Simple Syrup (recipe on page 29)
- 2 Fresh Basil Leaves
- Ice
- Lemon wheel for garnish

PREPARATION

1. Put ice in the shaker until it is halfway full.
2. Pour the lemon juice.
3. Add the basil leaves and basil syrup.
4. Shake well.
5. Pour into a martini glass and garnish with the lemon wheel.
6. Enjoy!

SCAN ME

BASIL ORGEAT MOCKTAIL

INGREDIENTS

- 1.5 oz. Orgeat syrup (recipe on page 30)
- 1.5 oz. Lemon juice
- 5 Basil leaves
- 3 oz. Sparkling Mineral Water
- Mint spring and lemon wheel for garnish

PREPARATION

1. Pour the orgeat syrup, lemon juice and four basil leaves into a shaker and shake it up.
2. Take a large leave of basil and put it at the bottom of the glass and cover it with crushed ice.
3. Double strain the mix into the glass.
4. Top it off with soda water and stir.
5. Garnish with a lemon wheel.
6. Enjoy!

SCAN ME

CHAI DIGESTIVE MOCKTAIL

INGREDIENTS

- 1 oz. Masala Chai Syrup (recipe on page 31)
- 1 Orange squeezed
- ½ oz. Apple cider vinegar
- 1-2 dashes of orange bitters
- ¼ cup of Ginger ale
- Ice
- Orange wheel and a cinnamon stick for garnish.

PREPARATION

1. Peel the orange and squeeze the peel into the glass
2. Add Ice
3. Add the masala chai syrup, orange juice, apple cider vinegar and drops of orange bitters.
4. Stir it well.
5. Top with ginger ale.
6. Garnish with an orange wheel and a cinnamon stick.
7. Enjoy!

SCAN ME

CHRISTMAS MOCKTAIL

INGREDIENTS

- 1 oz. Rosemary Maple Syrup (recipe on page 32)
- 2 oz. Cranberry juice
- ½ oz. Apple Cider Vinegar
- ½ cup of Ginger Ale
- Spring of fresh rosemary to garnish

PREPARATION

1. Add ice into a glass.
2. Add rosemary maple syrup, cranberry juice and apple cider vinegar.
3. Top it with the Ginger Ale and stir.
4. Garnish with the spring of fresh rosemary.
5. Enjoy!

SCAN ME

CUCUMBER MOCKTAIL

INGREDIENTS

- 4 slices of cucumber
- 4-6 mint leaves
- ½ oz. Simple Syrup (recipe on page 27)
- 1 oz. fresh lime juice
- Ice
- 2-3 oz. Sparkling Mineral Water
- Sprig of mint and slice of cucumber for garnish

PREPARATION

1. Put the cucumber slices, mint leaves, simple syrup and fresh lime juice.
2. Give it a quick muddle.
3. Add a little bit of crushed ice.
4. Pour the sparkling water.
5. Give it a little stir.
6. Garnish with mint leaves and a slice of cucumber.
7. Enjoy!

SCAN ME

GRAPEFRUIT MOCKTAIL

INGREDIENTS

- 4 oz. Grapefruit Juice
- 2 oz. Lemon Juice
- Ice
- 1 Large Orange
- ½ oz. of Honey Simple Syrup (Dilute honey with warm water, 2:1 ratio)
- ½ oz. of Rose Water
- ½ Cup of Soda Water
- 1 Lemon wheel and spring of mint for garnish

PREPARATION

1. Add the grapefruit juice and lemon juice into a shaker.
2. Add Ice and shake it.
3. Add the rose water and syrup.
4. Shake it for 5-10 seconds.
5. Pour it and top it with soda water.
6. Garnish with a lemon wheel and a spring of mint.
7. Enjoy!

SCAN ME

LEMON THYME MOCKTAIL

INGREDIENTS

- 1 Lemon
- 4-7 fresh mint leaves
- 4 Springs of fresh thyme
- ½ oz. Honey diluted with ½ oz. of water
- ¾ Cup of Lemon Kombucha

PREPARATION

1. In a shaker add lemons peeled, the mint leaves and thyme.
2. Muddle it to take out the flavors and shake it well.
3. Add ice into a glass and pour the mixture.
4. Add the honey water and top it with the lemon kombucha.
5. Garnish with a lemon wheel and the thyme spring.
6. Enjoy!

SCAN ME

ORANGE EXPLOSION

INGREDIENTS

- ½ cup of Ice
- ½ oz. Mango juice
- 1 oz. Red grape juice
- ½ oz. Orange juice
- 1 Cup of soda Water
- 1 orange slice to garnish

PREPARATION

1. Take a cocktail shaker and fill it with ice.
2. Add the fresh orange juice, mango juice and grape juice.
3. Shake well.
4. Strain into a martini glass.
5. Top with club soda.
6. Garnish with an orange wheel.

SCAN ME

PEAR & ROSE PUNCH

INGREDIENTS

- 1l pear juice
- 1 vanilla pod
- 1 oz. sugar
- 4 Cardamom pods
- Few slices of fresh ginger
- 1 oz. Apple cider vinegar
- ½ oz. Rosewater
- 8-9 oz. Sparkling water
- Ice
- 2-3 Rosemary sprigs
- 2 Sliced red pears.
- Handful frozen redcurrants

STEP 1

1. Into a pan, pour the pear juice. Add the vanilla, sugar, cardamom and ginger. Bring it to a simmer. After 10 minutes remove from heat and let it cool down completely.

STEP 2

1. In a pitcher, pour the juice, the apple cider vinegar, rosewater and sparkling water. Then add ice and stir well.
2. Add slices of red pear, frozen red currants and rosemary sprigs.
3. Serve and enjoy!

SCAN ME

VIRGIN SANGRIA

INGREDIENTS

- 2 cups of ice
- 2 oranges
- 1 oz. Lemon juice
- 1 Cup of Strawberries
- 1 Apple cut in slices

- ½ cup of cherries
- 3 cups of Sprite
- 2 cups Grape juice
- 5 basil leaves

PREPARATION

1. Grab a pitcher and add the ice.
2. Add the oranges sliced.
3. Add the juice from the lemon.
4. Add the strawberries.
5. Add the apple, cut into slices.
6. Add the cherries.
7. Add the grape juice.
8. Add the Sprite.
9. Add the Basil and stir well.
10. Let it rest in the fridge for 1 hour

SCAN ME

PINEAPPLE & GINGER PUNCH

INGREDIENTS

- 750ml Pineapple juice
- 1 oz. Lime juice
- 2 Small bunch of mint, woody stalks removed
- Ice
- 2 cups of ginger beer
- Mint to garnish

PREPARATION

1. Pour the pineapple juice and lime juice into a blender. Add the mint and a couple of handfuls of ice, then blitz until the ice is crushed.
2. Put the mix into tumblers filled with more ice, then top up with the ginger beer.
3. Garnish each glass with mint and star anise.
4. Enjoy!

SCAN ME

POMEGRANATE MOJITO MOCKTAIL

INGREDIENTS

- 1 tbsp pomegranate seeds
- Big bunch mint
- ½ oz. Lime juice
- ½ Cup of pomegranate juice
- ¼ Cup of lemonade

PREPARATION

1. A day ahead, divide the pomegranate seeds between the holes in an ice cube tray, top up with water and freeze.
2. Add the lime and mint into a shaker
3. Muddle it to take out the flavors
4. Pour the Pomegranate juice and lemonade and give it a shake.
5. Add the ice cubes with the pomegranate seeds into a glass.
6. Strain the pomegranate mix
7. Garnish with a lime slice and mint spring.
8. Enjoy!

SCAN ME

SAGE SOUR MOCKTAIL

INGREDIENTS

- 2 oz. Tonic water
- 1 oz. Lemon juice
- ½ oz. Simple syrup (recipe on page 27)
- 4 Sage leaves
- Ice
- ½ oz. Egg white

PREPARATION

1. Put the lemon juice, syrup, tonic water, sage leaves and ice into a shaker.
2. Shake it well.
3. Take out the ice and the sage.
4. Add egg white.
5. Shake it firmly for 10-15 seconds. This will create the froth from the egg white.
6. Pour the mixture into a cocktail glass.
7. Garnish with a sage leaf.
8. Enjoy!

SCAN ME

THE ITALIAN MOCKTAIL

INGREDIENTS

- Ice
- 1 Spring of Rosemary
- 1 oz. Peach Nectar
- 1 oz. Cranberry Juice
- ½ oz. Fresh Orange Juice
- ½ oz. Simple syrup (recipe on page 27)
- ½ cup of Sparkling water
- 1 Orange wheel and Rosemary spring for garnish.

PREPARATION

1. On a shaker add ice, one sprig of rosemary, the simple syrup, orange juice, cranberry juice and peach nectar.
2. Shake well.
3. Strain into a glass with some ice.
4. Top with sparkling water.
5. Garnish with the spring of rosemary and an orange wheel.
6. Enjoy!

SCAN ME

VIRGIN PINEAPPLE MOCKTAIL

INGREDIENTS

- ½ oz. Orange juice
- ½ oz. Simple syrup (recipe on page 27)
- 2 oz. Pineapple juice
- Ice
- ½ Cup of Soda Water
- Lime slice for garnish

PREPARATION

1. Take a cocktail shaker and fill it with the ice
2. Pour the orange juice, simple syrup and pineapple juice.
3. Shake well
4. Pour it into a glass
5. Top with Soda Water
6. Garnish with a slice of lime
7. Enjoy!

SCAN ME

EARL GREY MOCKTAIL

INGREDIENTS

- 1 oz. Lemon juice
- 1 oz. Earl grey syrup (recipe on page 33)
- 3/4 oz. Aquafaba (or chickpea water)
- 2-3 oz. Tonic Water
- Lemon slice and spring mint for garnish

PREPARATION

1. Into a shaker combine the earl gray syrup, lemon juice and aquafaba.
2. Give it a dry shake (no ice) to make the froth.
3. Into a collins glass with ice pour a bit of tonic water on the bottom (around 1oz).
4. Strain the mix into the ice.
5. Top it off with tonic water.
6. Garnish with a lemon slice and a mint leaf.
7. Enjoy!

SCAN ME

APPLE MINT MOJITO

INGREDIENTS

- 1 oz. Green Apple Syrup (recipe on page 34)
- ½ oz. Mint Syrup (recipe on page 16)
- 1 oz. Lime Juice
- 4-5 Mint Leaves
- Soda Water
- Ice Cubes
- Mint spring and a slice of apple for garnish.

PREPARATION

1. Pour green apple syrup, mint syrup and lime juice.
2. Muddle it to take out the flavors.
3. Add ice cubes.
4. Fill up with soda water and stir well.
5. Garnish with a spring of mint and a slice of apple.
6. Enjoy!

SCAN ME

ASIAN SOUR MOCKTAIL

INGREDIENTS

- ½ oz. Passion fruit Syrup (recipe on page 35)
- 2 oz. Brewed Lemongrass Tea
- ½ oz. Lemon juice
- ½ oz. Egg white
- Ice Cubes

PREPARATION

1. Combine ingredients in a shaker and dry shake
2. Then put ice cubes into a shaker and shake again
3. Double strain
4. Pour mixture into chilled glass
5. Top it with the foam and a slice of lemon.
6. Enjoy!

SCAN ME

CLEMENTINE MOJITO MOCKTAIL

INGREDIENTS

- 4 oz. Clementine juice
- ½ oz. Demerara sugar
- 1 lemon wheel
- ½ cup of clementine slices
- Ice
- 4-6 mint leaves
- ½ oz. Orange Blossom water
- 3 oz of Sparkling water

PREPARATION

1. Pour the juice into a glass and stir in the sugar.
2. Tip in the chopped clementine and lemon wheel, then crush using a muddler.
3. Add a handful of ice, the mint and orange blossom.
4. Top up slowly with sparkling water and stir well.
5. Garnish with a clementine slice
6. Enjoy!

SCAN ME

FALL FIG MOCKTAIL

INGREDIENTS

- 1 Fig
- 8 Mint Leaves
- 1/2 oz. Brown Sugar
- 4 oz. Ginger Ale
- Ice
- Mint spring for garnish

PREPARATION

1. Muddle the fig, brown sugar, and 7 mint leaves in a shaker until the fig is well broken down.
2. Add ginger ale to the shaker and stir until combined.
3. Strain and pour into a glass over ice.
4. Garnish with the last mint leaf and any leftover figs.
5. Enjoy!

SCAN ME

FIG LIME MOCKTAIL

INGREDIENTS

- ½ oz. Lime juice
- 1 oz. Fig syrup (recipe on page 36)
- 3 oz. Club soda
- Ice
- 1 Fig and lavender spring for garnish

PREPARATION

1. Mix the syrup, club soda, and lime in a cocktail mixing cup.
2. Add a cocktail ice cube.
3. Top it with club soda.
4. Garnish with a fig and lavender spring.
5. Enjoy!

SCAN ME

FRUIT MIX TEA

INGREDIENTS

- ½ oz. Orange Syrup (recipe on page 18)
- ¼ oz. Strawberry Syrup(recipe on page 28)
- 1 ½. oz. Apple juice
- 100 ml Brewed Black Tea
- Ice
- Rosemary spring for garnish

PREPARATION

1. Pour all ingredients into a shaker then add some ice cubes.
2. Shake well around 5-10 seconds.
3. Strain into a Collins glass with ice.
4. Garnish with a rosemary spring.
5. Enjoy!

SCAN ME

PASSION FRUIT MARTINI MOCKTAIL

INGREDIENTS

- ½ cup Passion fruit juice
- 1 oz. Lemon juice
- 1 oz. Egg white
- 1 oz. Simple syrup (recipe on page 27)
- Ice
- Sparkling grape juice
- Slice of lime for garnish

PREPARATION

1. Into a shaker add the passion fruit juice, lemon juice, egg white and simple syrup and give it a dry shake for 15 seconds.
2. Add the ice, then shake again until the outside of the shaker feels cold.
3. Double strain into a martini glass.
4. Top it with the grape juice and top some of the foam left on the shaker.
5. Garnish with a slice of lime.
6. Enjoy!

SCAN ME

PASSION FRUIT MOCKTAIL

INGREDIENTS

- 4 Passion fruits
- 2.5 oz. Simple Syrup (recipe on page 27)
- Soda Water
- Ice
- Rosemary spring for garnish

PREPARATION

1. Take the inside of the passion fruit and put it into a blender.
2. Add the simple syrup.
3. Pulse for about 1 minute until the fruit is completely blended.
4. Put ice cubes in a glass.
5. Strain some of the mixture.
6. Top off with Soda Water.
7. Add a rosemary spring.
8. Enjoy!

SCAN ME

PIÑA COLADA

INGREDIENTS

- 1 oz. Mango Syrup
- 2 oz. Coconut milk
- 1 oz. Apple juice
- ½ cup Pineapple Fruit (slices)
- Ice Cubes

PREPARATION

1. Pour all ingredients into a blender then add some ice cubes.
2. Blend until smooth.
3. Pour the mix into a glass.
4. Garnish with a slice of pineapple and a spring of mint.
5. Enjoy!

SCAN ME

SPARKLING PEACH PUNCH

INGREDIENTS

- 3 cups of Brewed green tea
- 5 large ripe peaches
- 1 oz. Lime juice
- 5 cups of Ginger Ale
- 2 oz. Agave nectar
- 5-7 Mint leaves

PREPARATION

1. Blend 4 peaches and lime juice until smooth.
2. In a pitcher add ice, 1 peach into slices, the peach juice, green tea and agave nectar.
3. Top it with ginger ale and add mint leaves.
4. Stir well.
5. Enjoy!

SCAN ME

STRAWBERRY BELLINI MOCKTAIL

INGREDIENTS

- 4 to 6 Large Fresh Strawberries
- 1 oz. Lime juice
- 20 ml Strawberry Syrup (recipe on page 28)
- 20 ml Simple Syrup (recipe on page 27)
- Soda Water
- Ice Cubes
- 1 Half strawberry for garnish

PREPARATION

1. Put the strawberry, strawberry syrup, simple syrup, lime juice, and ice cubes into a blender.
2. Blend until smooth.
3. Pour Blended ingredients into a chilled glass.
4. Top with soda water.
5. Garnish with a strawberry.
6. Enjoy!

SCAN ME

ZUCCHINI MOCKTAIL

INGREDIENTS

- 4 oz. Zucchini Juice
- 1 oz. Raw Honey
- 1 oz. Lemon juice
- Ice Cubes
- Zucchini or cucumber wheel for garnish

PREPARATION

1. Blend zucchini with water (2:1 ratio).
2. Strain through a fine-mesh strainer the juice.
3. Pour all ingredients into the shaker, including the ice.
4. Shake well and strain into chilled glass.
5. Garnish.
6. Enjoy!

SCAN ME

CONVERSION CHART
MEASURMENTS

Cup	Ounces	Milliliters
1 Cup	8 oz	240 ml
3/4 Cup	6 oz	177 ml
2/3 Cup	5 oz	158 ml
1/2 Cup	4 oz	118 ml
3/8 Cup	3 oz	90 ml
1/3 Cup	2.5 oz	79 ml
1/4 Cup	2 oz	59 ml
1/8 Cup	1 oz	30 ml
1/16 Cup	1/2 oz	15 ml

WEIGHT

Imperial	Metric
1/2 oz	15 g
1 oz	29 g
2 oz	57 g
3 oz	85 g
4 oz	113 g
5 oz	141 g
6 oz	170 g
8 oz	227 g
10 oz	283 g

CONCLUSION

In conclusion, these mocktail recipes are sure to be a hit at your next party or gathering! Whether you're looking for something fruity, refreshing, or even a little bit decadent, there's a recipe here that will fit the bill. So go ahead and mix up a batch of your favorites and enjoy!

If you have liked this book and found these recipes original and refreshing make sure to leave a review! It will help us create more books and delicious recipes.

Cheers!

Made in the USA
Monee, IL
12 October 2024

67767602R00052